DIGITAL COLOR WHEEL

C O P Y R I G H T

Glenn Calhoun
!00 South Jefferson Avenue
Wenonah, New Jersey 08090
glenncalhoun@comcast.net

Copyright ® 2016 by Glenn Calhoun

ISBN - 13: 978-1539819639
ISBN -10: 1539819639

The author has done everything possible to make this textbook accurate, up to date, and in accord with accepted standards at the time of the publication. The author is not responsible for errors or omissions in this textbook. The reader is advised always to check for program changes and new information regarding the operation of computer programs such as the one used to create this RGB color wheel.

HOW TO CREATE A
DIGITAL COLOR WHEEL
A STEP BY STEP PROCESS
IN ADOBE ILLUSTRATOR

BY GLENN CALHOUN

D E D I C A T I O N

I have made some rough calculations and believe
that so far in my career, I have taught over 14,000
graphic design students. There has never been a day,
a class, or a student that has been a problem.
Therefore, I am dedicating this textbook to the
14,000 plus and a very special thank you to my
two bestfriends, my wife Cindy and my son Sam.

A B O U T T H E A U T H O R

Glenn Calhoun is a graduate of Thomas Edison
State University, with related technical studies at
Pratt Institute of Technology Degree classes,
Delaware County College Business classes,
University of Pittsburgh Liberal Arts field of study,
Ivy School of Professional Fine Art and graphics, and
the Art Institute of Pittsburgh. Currently he is ranked
first in seniority at the Art Institute of Philadelphia
College and teaches the Adobe suite programs
as well as fundamentals of design and advertising.
His approach to teaching is unique in that his goal
is for those around him to experience the acquisition
of knowledge in a manner that has permanence
for the individual. He believes that lessons learned
and then forgotten, are lessons that have not
been taught so they have interest.

Mr. Calhoun is not only a teacher he is a
medical illustrator using traditional media skills,
a graphic designer using the Adobe platforms, a
computer illustrator, a fabricator of complex
packaging, a muralist, a curriculum developer, and
writer. He enjoys developing answers to complex
objectives, so that they are easily understood. It is not
all work and no play that motivates Mr. Calhoun.
Family, friends and community are as much apart of
his life as is his endless desire to create.

F O R W A R D

The *Chicago Manual of Style*, states that the forward of a textbook should be written by someone other than the editor or the author. Because this is the first publication of *How to Create a Digital Color Wheel*, I thought it might be interesting to offer my readers a chance to be the forward authors. These individuals, with their permission, will have their comments accompanied by their names and these will serve as the forward for the next printing of the textbook.

Individuals interested in have their reviews published along with their names and occupations should email glenncalhoun@comcast.net. Title your comments for submission "RGB forward".

P R E F A C E

Graphic designers and design educators face many common challenges in their professions. First, although it is not normal for any working professional in the field of graphic design, advertising, fashion, web design, interior design, game design, or animation to have the responsibility of creating a color wheel, it is certainly a key element in the training needed to function properly in one of the aforementioned commercial environments. The foundations of color, in commercial art, begin with traditional skills. One of the first skills practiced is the creation of a color wheel using paint as the medium. Second, due to the expansion of computer technology there is a need to teach and understand color beyond the traditional, reflective colors used to create a basic color wheel. There is now a need to educate the students entering a training directive focused on a career in a commercial field of art, in the creation of a different kind of color wheel. The new style of color wheel needed, is transmitted color and this wheel must be created in an RGB based platform.

Due to the fact that the vast majority of textbooks lack image support for the text based messages, and training videos are difficult to follow even though they offer a sequential message, I recognized the need for something different. Therefore, in order to instruct students and assist my professional colleagues in this Adobe Illustrator based process, on how to create an RGB color wheel, I developed an image based, copy supported process.

Jean Calhoun

07-07-2016

A C K N O W L E D G M E N T S

I would like to acknowledge and extend a special thanks to the students, faculty, and graphic design professionals that tested, read, and edited the manuscripts before printing. I would like to send a special thanks to those who were brave enough to provide detailed ideas and evaluations, that became valuable contributions used in improving the textbook.

The objective of this publication is to enable the reader to follow a step by step process thats results in the creation of a digital color wheel. Steps used to create the color wheel are presented with number or letter sequential guides. Readers are cautioned when there is the potential to error in the process. The development of the color wheel starts out using a CMYK platform for an easier production process. After the construction of the colorless wheel is made, the color platform is changed to RGB. The finished RGB color wheel is a digital color wheel and the objective of the textbook.

Q U O T E

"It's only rain."

– Allen Felton

HOW TO CREATE A
DIGITAL COLOR WHEEL
A STEP BY STEP PROCESS

This book guides the reader by way of a one sided conversation. All the material is presented in a casual manner. Little points of interest that make the readers task easier are noted. Directions are visual, rather than text only, complexities are featured, and at points the user is told, "be-careful". Text and visuals clearly present key parts of the Illustrator program used and are based on the concept, that individuals reading the directions have only a basic understanding of the program, even though creating a digital color wheel for most seasoned professionals would be a complex and unwanted task.

GLENN CALHOUN 2016

After Illustrator is launched select File > New.
The New Document panel appears on screen.

Name the document.

Set Units to Inches.

One Artboard will be enough.

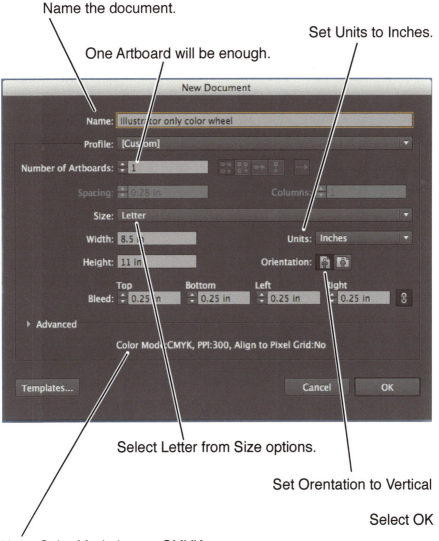

Select Letter from Size options.

Set Orentation to Vertical

Select OK

Note: Color Mode is now CMYK.
This will change, because this is a digital color wheel (RGB).
CMYK colors are reflective (printed) colors that use,
Blue, Red, Yellow, & Black inks.

First, launch some of the most important tools/panels
and bring them in close to the art board.

Select the Elipse Tool from the Tool Bar.
It is hidden under the Rectangle Tool.   Swatches panel

Create a large Circle (Shift + Drag Mouse).

Align panel

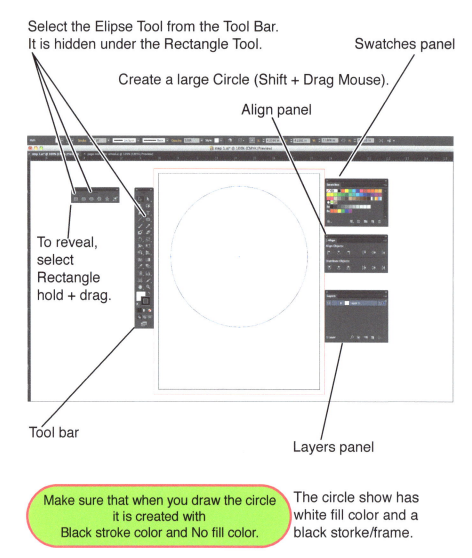

To reveal,
select
Rectangle
hold + drag.

Tool bar

Layers panel

Make sure that when you draw the circle
it is created with
Black stroke color and No fill color.

The circle show has
white fill color and a
black storke/frame.

NOTE: All of the panels can be found under Window.
Remove/close all other panels.

1. Make sure that No Fill and Black Stroke are selected.

   2. Now that you have the circle drawn and it is selected,
      go to the Align panel:

      5. Go to Window at the top of your screen, select
            Object > Path > Offset Path.

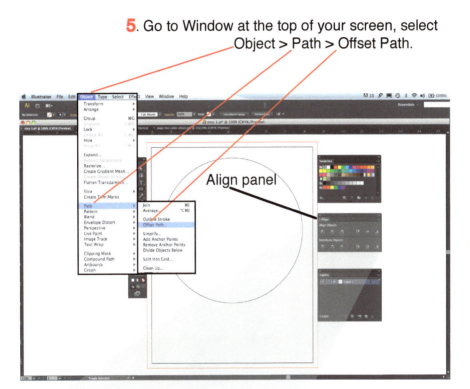

Align panel

3. Select Vertical Align Center.

4. Select Horizonal Align Center.

Note: Make sure to follow the steps.

Now to create the inner circle of the color wheel.

With the large circle selected, select Object > Path > Offset Path.
The Offset Path panel appears.

1. Change Offset measurement to -1 in.

2. Select Preview.

3. Select OK.

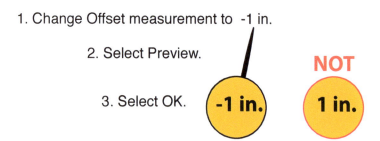

NOT

-1 in.   1 in.

1. Double click the words "Layer 1" and change it to 'C-wheel'.

2. Select the bottom right corner (folded corner icon) to create a new layer. Name this layer 'Wheel pieces' using the same process as Layer 1.

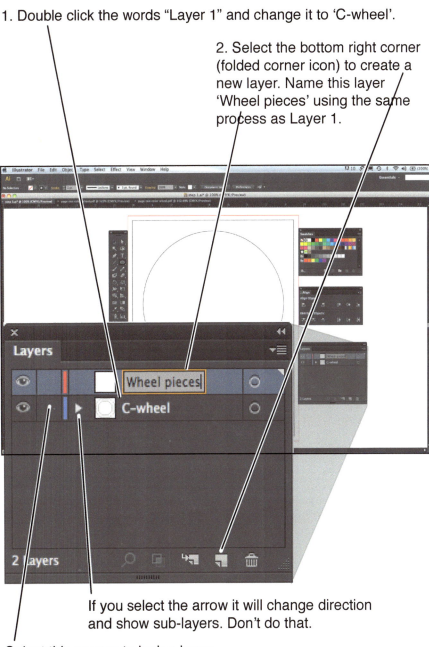

If you select the arrow it will change direction and show sub-layers. Don't do that.

Select this square to lock a layer.
Editabled when not locked.

1. Use the Selection Tool and select any point on the outer circle.
   The center point will be visible.
   Mark the center using guides.

      2.Click and drag guides to mark the center of the circles.

      3. Lock the C-wheel layer.   4. Select Wheel pieces layer.

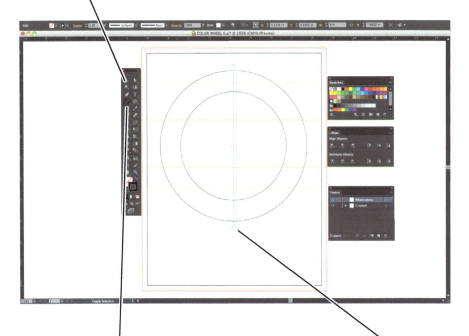

5. With the Wheel pieces layer
   selected. Select the
   Line Segment Tool. Move the
   curser to the center of the circle,
   press option + shift and drag
   the mouse at the same time.

6. Make a line that extends beyond
   the edges of the largest circle.

Guides
A. To create guides, first select
command > R.
Rulers appear.

B. Place the curser in the top ruler area,
   click and drag guide from the top down.
C. Next, from left ruler, drag guide right.

1. Move the cursor to the Tool Bar and select the Rotation Tool.

2. Double click the Rotation Tool icon.

3. The Rotate panel appears. When you open the Rotate panel the line on the circle may move.
Don't panic, it's OK.

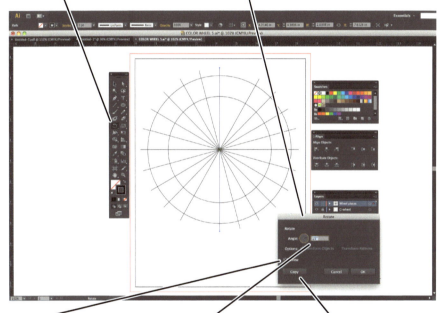

A. If preview is not selected at this point, it is not a big deal.

B. Change Angle to 15.

C. Now turn on the Prievew.

D. Select Copy.

E. Now for the big step. Press the command key plus D again, again, and again, filling the circle with spokes.

Note: Make sure you follow the numbered steps in sequence.
You now have 24 pie wedges, 24 slices made, or 12 cut lines, take your pick.

1. Go to the Layers panel,
   Click the target on Wheel pieces layer.
   This selects every slice.

2. Select Object > Group.

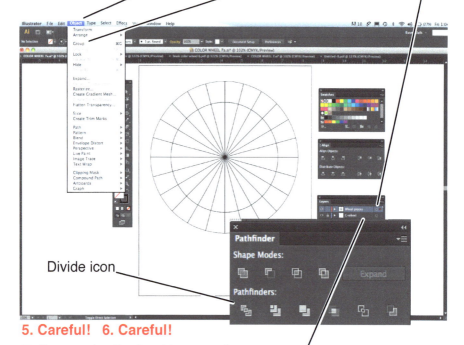

Divide icon

5. Careful!   6. Careful!

7. Stay on the C-wheel layer and
   Command + Click the layer target.
   Next, Command + Click the target
   on the Wheel pieces layer.

8. Go to the Pathfinder panel,
   located in Window drop menu.
   Select the Divide icon in the
   Pathfinders section of the
   Pathfinder panel.

3. Go back to layers panel.
   Go to the C-wheel layer
   and click the target.

4. Go to the lock
   on the C-wheel layer
   and unlock the layer, if
   it is locked.

9. Each piece is now an individual piece.

Removing things that are not needed.

1. Go to the Layers panel.
   Unlock the Wheel pieces layer, if locked.
   Unlock the C-wheel layer also, if locked.

2. Click the eye on the
   C-wheel layer and
   turn it off.

3. Select the arrow on the
   layer containing the pieces.
   A sub-layer appears,
   titled Group.

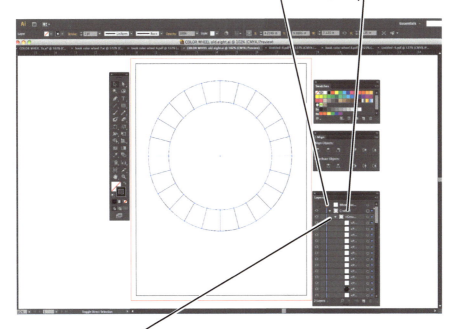

4. Select the arrow
   on the layer named
   Group. This reveals
   over 40 sub-layers.

5. Scroll down until you come in
   contact with the first visual
   triangle. Look close, they are
   very faint images.

6. Select on the first visible triangle
   and highlight the layer.

7. Scroll down to the last triangle
   and Shift > Click. This selects
   the layer and layers in between.

8. Move the curser to trash can
   and click. Mission accomplished.

If you have missed a triangle, find it by turning the eyes off and on.

A new word, 'keystone'.
A keystone shape, is a wedge shaped piece of an apex, of in an arch.
The circle created is made up of 24 separate keystone pieces.

At this point, the 24 keystone pieces are not grouped. To create a good color wheel, the foundation color piece (RED), should be centered at the top of the color wheel.

1. Select all 24 pieces by selecting the target on the layer showing the 24 pieces.

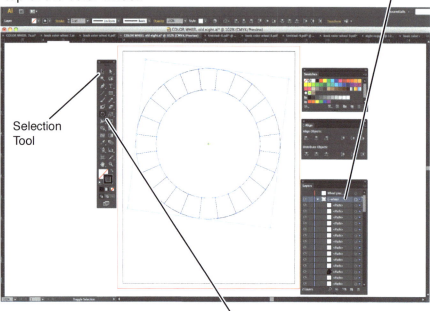

Selection
Tool

2. Go to Object > Group.

3. Select the Rotate Tool from the Tool Bar, using the Selection Tool.

4. Rotate the wheel so that the center point of one keystone is the center line of the overall circle. Sounds complex. It's not, just put a keystone shape at the top. Click to move and center the shape.

5. Go to Object > Ungroup.

Now to start adding color.
This wheel will be created in RGB palette (transmitted colors).
Web colors are based on red, green, and blue, transmitted color.

1. The CMYK swatches can no longer be used.
   So the hunt is on for the RGB swatch panel.

Window

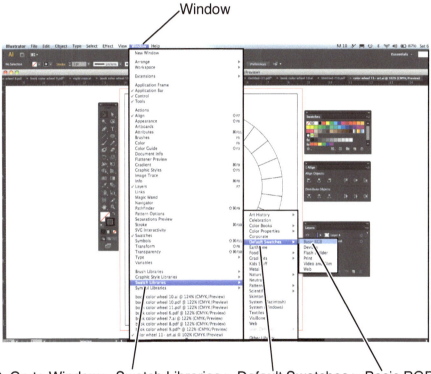

2. Go to Window > Swatch Libraries > Default Swatches > Basic RGB.

NOTE: In order to add color to the blank color wheel the wheel must be ungrouped. This can be done by selecting all of the wheel, and then going to Object > Ungroup.

When the wheel is ungrouped you can select on any section with the Selection Tool in order to highlight it or move it.

In order to highlight a keystone shape and add color, select on the top edge or bottom edge of the keystone shape.

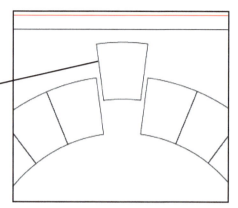

This is the image that will appear when the Large List View is selected from the Basic RGB panel.

Select on this corner to reveal the option section of the RGB panel.

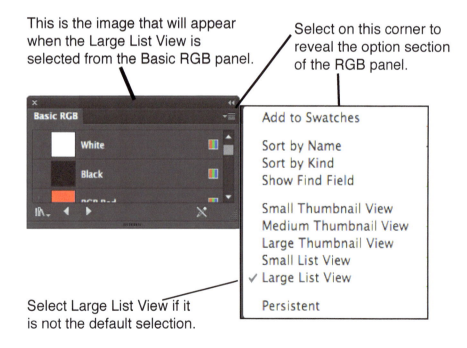

Select Large List View if it is not the default selection.

Extend the Basic RGB panel to a point where the primary colors
are visible. Further is OK.

   Here are the first set of steps to follow.
      1. Select the top, of the top center keystone.
         Use the Selection Tool.
      2. Make sure Fill color is on top in the tool bar (white or no fill).
      3. Make sure that the Stroke has no color (red stripe).
      4. Move the Selection Tool to the Basic RGB panel
         and select on RGB Red.   Bingo!   You are on your way.

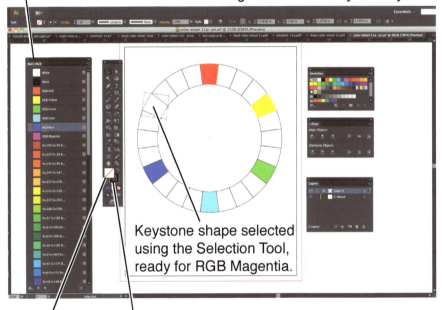

Keystone shape selected
using the Selection Tool,
ready for RGB Magentia.

Fill color
(now showing None).

Stroke color
(now showing Black).
Note: Stroke will need to be changed to None.

   5. Select the fourth keystone to the right
      of the, now red keystone.
   6. Click on RGB Yellow in the
      Basic RGB panel with the Selection Tool.

   7. Keep going, next Green, then Cyan, then
      Blue, and the sixth color is Magenta.

Now that the light source primary colors (digital red, yellow, blue)
and the secondary colors (yellow, cyan, magenta)
are constructed using the Basic RGB color panel,
convert the entire file/document to RGB by selecting,
File > Document Color Mode > RGB Color.

This change will show up in the
document preview bar when saved.

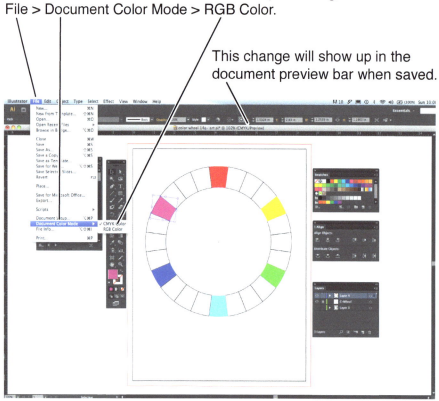

Filling the remaining segments of the color wheel.

1. Draw a large rectangle as shown, use
   the Rectangler Tool in the tool bar (no stroke).
   2. Select the rectangle, then select
      the Eyedropper Tool in the tool bar.
      3. Move the eyedropper to the red keystone shape in the
         color wheel and select. The rectangle will fill with the
         same red as the color wheel.

Eyedropper Tool

4. Draw an ellipse as shown (no stroke).
   Use the Ellipse Tool in the tool bar.
   5. Fill the ellipse with yellow from the color wheel.
      In order to fill the ellipse with color, use the same process
      as filling the rectangle with color.

Developing the colors between the Primary and Secondary colors.

Double click on the Blend Tool to reveal the Blend Options panel.

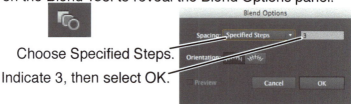

Choose Specified Steps.

Indicate 3, then select OK.

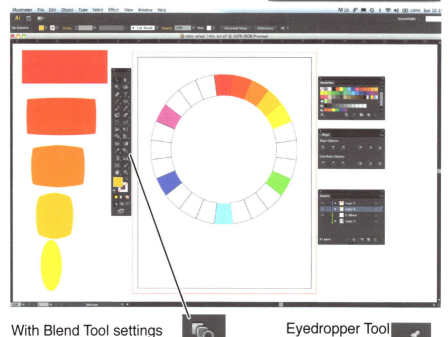

With Blend Tool settings made, follow these steps.

Eyedropper Tool

1. Using the Blend Tool, select the red rectangle and then select the yellow oval. This reveals a total of five colors.
2. Use the Selection Tool and select the blank keystone that touches the red keystone on the right side.
3. Select the Eyedropper Tool. Use this tool to select the color created using the Blend Tool, located directly under the largest rectangle. This action changes the keystone to the color selected.
4. Repet the process to fill the additional two keystones.

The Align panel and Swatches panel can be closed.

1. Select the large red rectangle with the Direct Selection Tool.
2. Select the Eyedropper Tool.
3. Select the Green keystone in the color wheel,
   with the Eyedropper Tool. This action creates the colors to be
   applied between Yellow and Green.
4. Follow the established process used the create the colors
   between Red and Yellow.

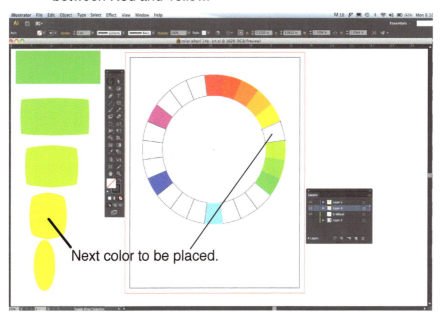

Next color to be placed.

Use caution this gets a little tricky.

1. This time select the the ellipse with the Direct Selection Tool.
2. Select the Eyedropper Tool.
3. Use the Eyepropper Tool to select on the Cyan keystone.
    This results in creating the next set of colors to be applied
    to the color wheel.

Here are the remaining steps.

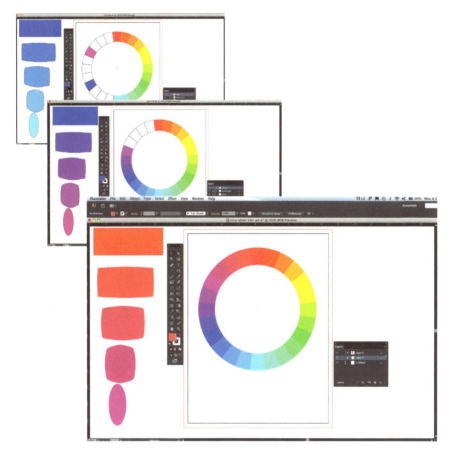

As a follow up:

Use the Zoom Tool to zoom in and check possible areas that may, do to some minor error, have a black frame that escaped. Select on the unwanted lines using the Direct Selection Tool and press delete.

Or, or, or, you can Select > All and apply None to the Stroke icon in the tool bar.

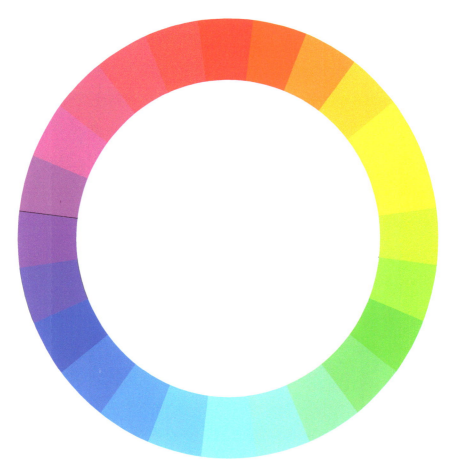

WELL DONE.

Do you like this style of training? InDesign got you down? Can't figure out how to make a compound path in Illustrator. Not even sure how a compound path will make your design life easier. Need the basics on how to create an interactive pdf? You're not the only one.

Send me a request. I will quote you a price per page and the number of pages needed to supplement your training on the subject, just like the digital color wheel.

Send your request to:
glenncalhoun@comcast.net
Title it, Training needed.

www.ingramcontent.com/pod-product-compliance
Lightning Source LLC
LaVergne TN
LVHW012317070326
832902LV00004BA/86